ENCOURAGE ME

ENCOURAGE ME

Charles R. Swindoll

MULTNOMAH PRESS
PORTLAND, OREGON 97266

Design by Greg Snyder

ENCOURAGE ME
© 1982 by Charles R. Swindoll, Inc.
Published by Multnomah Press
Portland, Oregon 97266
Printed in the United States of America

Library of Congress Cataloging in Publication Data

Swindoll, Charles R.
   Encourage me.

   1. Consolation.   I. Title.
BV4905.2.S9 1982   248.8'6   82-8029
ISBN 0-88070-002-5   AACR2
ISBN 0-930014-95-2(pbk.)

85 86 87 88 89 90 91 92 – 12 10 9 8 7 6 5

CONTENTS

Introduction 7

Part One: Encourage Me, Lord

Psalm 61:1-2 15
Searching for Shelter 17
You Are Important 23
You Are Not a Nobody 27
Call for Help 31
The Hammer, the File, and the
    Furnace 35
An Antidote for Weariness 37
"Final Descent . . . Commence Prayer" . 41

Part Two: Encourage . . . Me Lord?

Philippians 2:1-5 51
Take Time to Be Tender 53
A Bridge Called Credibility 57
Stay in Circulation 61
The Fine Art of Blowing It 65
The Heart of Encouragement 69
Dress Your Dreams in Denim 73
"The Opra Ain't Over" 77
Be an Encourager! 81

Conclusion 85

Introduction

Encourage me.

Maybe you haven't said it out loud in recent days. But chances are you have shaped the words in the silent hallways of your soul.

Encourage me. *Please.*

Maybe you haven't stopped anyone on the street and said that precise phrase. But if someone who cared enough looked close enough . . . they would see the words written in your frowning face, drooping shoulders, pleading eyes. They would hear the words echo in your unguarded comments and unsuppressed sighs.

If the truth were known, you're *craving* some encouragement. Looking for it. Longing for it. And probably grieving because you've found it in such short supply.

Am I right? Is that where you've been lately? Hibernating in the den of discouragement? Licking your wounds under some heavy, dark clouds that won't blow away? Thinking seriously about quitting the human race?

If so, you are undoubtedly running shy on reinforcement and affirmation these days. You are beginning to wonder not *when* relief is coming, but *if* it will ever come, right? Even though you may not feel like reading anything, I really believe these pages will help. I am writing them with people like you in mind . . . people who have begun to question their own words and to doubt their own worth. People who feel riveted to the valley where the sun seldom shines and others seldom care.

That's you, isn't it?

That's also *me* more often than you might guess. The long shadows of discouragement have often stretched across my path. Those times have been bittersweet— bitter at first, sweet later on. So I understand. I do not write out of sterile theory but out of reality. My pen has been dipped in a deep well. The ink has been dark and often cold. At such times I have struggled with a lack of self worth . . . a common battle waged in the valley.

Please let me slip in at this moment one significant truth: You are still valuable. You count. Yes, you. The "you" inside your skin who has your personality and your appearance. No matter what finally led you to where you are today, you're the one I'd like to talk to for awhile. Even though you feel necessary to no one and noticed by none, I'd still appreciate having a few words with you. Yes, even if you are dirty and guilty.

I have only one goal in mind: to encourage you.

You have become acquainted with disappointments, broken dreams, and disillusionment. Crisis seems to be your closest companion. Like a ten-pound sledge, your heartache has been pounding you dangerously near desperation. Unless I miss my guess, negativism and cynicism have crept in. You see little hope around the corner. As one wag put it, "The light at the end of the tunnel is the headlamp of an oncoming train." You are nodding in agreement, but probably not smiling. Life has become terribly unfunny.

Tired, stumbling, beaten, discouraged friend, take heart! The Lord God can and will lift you up. No pit is so deep that He is not deeper still. No valley so dark that the light of His truth cannot penetrate. In His own inscrutable way, He will use the insight of these few pages to bring back the one ingredient that has spilled out of your life. *Encouragement.*

If you miss it and need it and want it, read on. And oh—if you find it, by all means spread it!

Someone close by may be ready to give up the search.

Charles R. Swindoll

Part One:

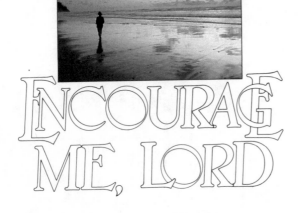

ENCOURAGE ME, LORD

"I cry tears
to you Lord
tears
because I cannot speak.
Words are lost
among my fears
pain
sorrows
losses
hurts
but tears
You understand
my wordless prayer
You hear.
Lord
wipe away my tears
all tears
not in distant day
but now
here."[1]

—Joseph Bayly

Hear my cry, O God;
listen to my prayer.
From the ends of the earth I call to
you,
I call as my heart grows faint;
lead me to the rock that is higher
than I.

(Psalm 61:1-2)

Searching for Shelter

Discouragement.

Where does it come from?

Sometimes it feels like a dry, barren wind off a lonely desert. And something inside us begins to wilt.

At other times it feels like a chilling mist. Seeping through our pores, it numbs the spirit and fogs the path before us.

What is it about discouragement that strips our lives of joy and leaves us feeling vulnerable and exposed?

I don't know all the reasons. I don't even know most of the reasons. But I do know *one* of the reasons: We don't have a refuge. Shelters are hard come by these days . . . you know, people who care enough to listen. Who are good at keeping secrets. And we all need harbors to pull into when we feel weather-worn and blasted by the storm.

I have an old Marine buddy who became a Christian several years after he was discharged from the Corps. When news of his conversion reached me, I was pleasantly surprised. He was one of those guys you'd never picture as being interested in spiritual things. He cursed loudly, drank heavily, fought hard, chased women, loved weapons, and hated chapel service. *He was a great marine.* But God? They weren't on speaking terms when I bumped around with him.

Then one day we ran into each other. As the conversation turned to his salvation, he frowned, put his hand on my shoulder, and made this admission:

Chuck, the only thing I miss is that old fellowship all the guys in our outfit used to have down at the slop shoot (Greek for tavern on base). *Man, we'd sit around, laugh, tell stories, drink a few beers, and really let our hair down. It was great! I just haven't found anything to take the place of that great time we used to enjoy. I ain't got nobody to admit my faults to . . . to have 'em put their arms around me and tell me I'm still okay.*

My stomach churned. Not because I was shocked, but because I had to agree. The man needed a refuge . . . someone to hear him out. The incident reminded me of something I read several months ago:

The neighborhood bar is possibly the best counterfeit there is to the fellowship Christ wants to give His church. It's an imitation, dispensing liquor instead of grace, escape rather than reality, but it is a permissive, accepting, and inclusive fellowship. It is unshockable. It is democratic. You can tell people secrets and they usually don't tell others or even want to. The bar flourishes not because most people are alcoholics, but because God has put into the human heart the desire to know and be known, to love and be loved, and so many seek a counterfeit at the price of a few beers.

With all my heart I believe that Christ wants His church to be . . . a fellowship where people can come in and say, "I'm sunk!" "I'm beat!" "I've had it!"[2]

Let me get painfully specific. Where do *you* turn when the bottom drops out of *your* life? Or when you face an issue that is embarrassing . . . maybe even scandalous. Like:

☐ You just discovered your son is a practicing homosexual.

☐ Your mate is talking separation or divorce.

☐ Your daughter has run away . . . for the fourth time. You are afraid she's pregnant.

☐ You've lost your job. It's your own fault.

☐ Financially, you've blown it.

☐ Your parent is an alcoholic.

☐   Your wife is having an affair.

☐   You flunked your entrance exam or you messed up the interview.

☐   You're in jail because you broke the law.

What do you need when circumstances puncture your fragile dikes and threaten to engulf your life with pain and confusion?

You need a shelter. A listener. Someone who understands.

But to whom do you turn when there's no one to tell your troubles to? Where do you find encouragement?

Without preaching, I'd like to call to your attention a man who turned to the living Lord and found in Him a place to rest and repair. His name? David. Cornered, bruised by adversity, and struggling with a low self-esteem, he wrote these words in his journal of woes:

In you, O LORD, I have taken refuge;
  let me never be put to shame;
  deliver me in your righteousness.
Turn your ear to me,
  come quickly to my rescue;
be my rock of refuge,
  a strong fortress to save me.   (Psalm 31:1-2)

Failing in strength and wounded in spirit, David cries out his need for a "refuge." The Hebrew term speaks of a protective place, a place of safety, security, secrecy. He tells the Lord that He—Jehovah God—became his refuge. In Him the troubled man found encouragement.

Now the question: Why do we need a refuge? As I read on through this psalm, I find three reasons unfolding:

First, because we are in distress and sorrow accompanies us.

Be merciful to me, O LORD, for I am in distress;
  my eyes grow weak with sorrow,
  my soul and my body with grief.
My life is consumed by anguish (vv. 9-10a).

Eyes get red from weeping. The heavy weights of sorrow press down. Depression, that serpent of despair, slithers silently through the soul's back door.

Depression is
Debilitating, defeating,
Deepening gloom.

Trudging wearily through
The grocery store,
Unable to make a simple choice,
Or to count out correct change.

Surveying an unbelievably messy house,
Piles of laundry,
Work undone, and not being
Able to lift a finger.

Doubting that God cares,
Doubting in my prayers,
Doubting He's even there.

Sitting, staring wild-eyed into space,
Desperately wanting out of the
human race.[3]

Heavy! But that's why we need a refuge.
Second, because we are sinful and guilt accuses us.

My strength fails because of my guilt
*   and my bones grow weak (v. 10b).*

There is shame between these lines.
Embarrassment. "It's my fault." What tough words to choke out! "I'm to blame."
An old British minister says it all when he writes:
This is the bitterest of all—to know that suffering need not have been; that it has resulted from indiscretion and inconsistency; that it is the harvest of one's own sowing; that the vulture which feeds on the vitals is a nestling of one's own rearing. Ah me! This is pain![4]
Harried and haunted by self-inflicted sorrow, we desperately search for a place to hide. But perhaps the most

devastating blow of all is dealt by others.

Third, because we are surrounded by adversaries and misunderstanding assaults us.

Because of all my enemies, I am the utter contempt
   of my neighbors;
I am a dread to my friends—
   those who see me on the street flee from me.
I am forgotten by them as though I were dead;
   I have become like broken pottery.
For I hear the slander of many;
   there is terror on every side;
they conspire against me
   and plot to take my life (vv. 11-13).

See how the hurting are handled?

"Utter contempt . . . a dread . . . those who see me flee from me . . . I am forgotten . . . I hear slander . . . there is terror . . . they conspire against me. . . ." Sound like a page out of your journal?

Tortured by the whisperings of others, we feel like a wounded, bleeding mouse in the paws of a hungry cat. The thought of what people are saying is more than we can bear. Gossip (even its name hisses) gives the final shove as we strive for balance at the ragged edge of despair.

Discouraged people don't need critics. They hurt enough already. They don't need more guilt or piled-on distress. They need encouragement. They need a refuge.

A place to hide and heal.

A willing, caring, available someone. A confidant and comrade-at-arms. Can't find one? Why not share David's shelter? The One he called My Strength, Mighty Rock, Fortress, Stronghold, and High Tower.

David's Refuge *never* failed. Not even once. And he never regretted the times he dropped his heavy load and ran for cover.

Neither will you.

You Are Important

There is only one YOU.

Think about that. Your face and features, your voice, your style, your background, your characteristics and peculiarities, your abilities, your smile, your walk, your handshake, your manner of expression, your viewpoint . . . everything about you is found in only one individual *since man first began*—YOU.

How does that make you feel? Frankly, I'm elated!

Dig as deeply as you please in the ancient, dusty archives of *Homo sapiens* and you'll not find another YOU in the whole lot. And that, by the way, did not "just happen"; it was planned that way. Why? Because God wanted you to be YOU, that's why. He designed you to be a unique, distinct, significant person unlike any other individual on the face of the earth, throughout the vast expanse of time. In your case, as in the case of every other human being, the mold was broken, never to be used again, once you entered the flow of mankind.

Listen to David's perspective on that subject:

You made all the delicate, inner parts of my body, and knit them together in my mother's womb. Thank you for making me so wonderfully complex! It is amazing to think about. Your workmanship is marvelous—and how well I know it. You were there while I was being formed in utter seclusion! You saw me before I was born and scheduled each day of my life before I began to breathe. Every day was recorded in your Book! (Psalm 139:13-16 TLB)

If I read this astounding statement correctly, you were prescribed and then presented to this world exactly as God arranged it. Reflect on that truth, discouraged friend. Read David's words one more time, and don't miss the comment that God is personally involved in the very days and details of your life. Great thought!

In our overly-populated, identity-crisis era, it is easy to forget this. Individuality is played down. We are asked to conform to the "system." Group opinion is considered superior to personal conviction and everything from the college fraternity to the businessman's service club tends to encourage our blending into the mold of the masses.

It's okay to "do your thing" just so long as it is similar to others when they do "their thing." Any other thing is the wrong thing. Hogwash!

This results in what I'd call an *image syndrome*, especially among the members of God's family called Christians. There is an "image" the church must maintain. The pastor (and his staff) should "fit the image" in the eyes of the public. So should all those in leadership. Youth programs and mission conferences and evangelistic emphases dare not drift too far from the expected image established back when. Nobody can say exactly when.

Our fellowship must be warm, but filled with clichés. Our love must be expressed, but not without its cool boundaries. The creative, free, and sometimes completely different approach so threatens the keepers of the "image syndrome" that one wonders how we retain *any* draft of fresh air blown through the windows of flexibility and spontaneity.

My mind lands upon a fig-picker from Tekoa . . . a rough, raw-boned shepherd who was about as subtle as a Mack truck on the Los Angeles-Santa Ana Freeway. He was tactless, unsophisticated, loud, uneducated, and uncooperative. His name was Amos. That was no problem. He was a preacher. That *was* a problem. He didn't fit the image . . . but he refused to let that bother him.

He was called (of all things) to bring the morning mes-
sages in the king's sanctuary. And bring them he did. His
words penetrated those vaulted ceilings and icy pews like
flaming arrows. In his own way, believing firmly in his
message, he pounced upon sin like a hen on a june bug . . .
and the "image keepers" of Israel told him to be silent, to
peddle his doctrine of doom in the backwoods of Judah.
His rugged style didn't fit in with the plush, "royal resi-
dence" at Bethel (Amos 7:12-13).

Aware of their attempt to strait-jacket his method and
restructure his message, Amos replied:

". . . I was neither a prophet nor a prophet's son, but I was a
shepherd, and I also took care of sycamore-fig trees. But the
LORD took me from tending the flock and said to me, 'Go,
prophesy to my people Israel' " (Amos 7:14-15).

Amos was not about to be something he wasn't! God
made him, God called him, and God gave him a message
to be communicated in his own, unique way. A Tekoa
High dropout had no business trying to sound or look like
a Princeton grad.

Do I write to an Amos? You don't "fit the mold"? Is that
what sent you down into the valley of discouragement?
You don't *sound* like every other Christian or *look* like the
"standard" saint . . . or *act* like the majority?

Hallelujah! Don't sweat it, my friend. And don't you
dare change just because you're outnumbered. Then you
wouldn't be YOU.

What the church needs is a lot more faithful figpickers
who have the courage to simply be themselves, regardless.
Whoever is responsible for standardizing the ranks of
Christians ought to be shot at dawn. In so doing they completely ignored the value of variety, which God planned
for His church when He *"arranged the parts in the body,
every one of them, just as He wanted them to be"* (1 Corinthians 12:18).

You are YOU. There is only one YOU. And YOU are important.

Want to start feeling better? Really desire to dispel discouragement? I can say it all in three words:

Start being YOU.

You Are Not a Nobody

We haven't gotten very far, but it's already time for a quiz.

Pull a sheet of scratch paper out of your memory bank and see how well you do with the following questions:

1. Who taught Martin Luther his theology and inspired his translation of the New Testament?

2. Who visited Dwight L. Moody at a shoe store and spoke to him about Christ?

3. Who worked alongside and encouraged Harry Ironside as his associate pastor?

4. Who was the wife of Charles Haddon Spurgeon?

5. Who was the elderly woman who prayed faithfully for Billy Graham for over twenty years?

6. Who financed William Carey's ministry in India?

7. Who refreshed the apostle Paul in that Roman dungeon as he wrote his last letter to Timothy?

8. Who helped Charles Wesley get underway as a composer of hymns?

9. Who found the Dead Sea Scrolls?

10. Who personally taught G. Campbell Morgan, the "peerless expositor," his techniques in the pulpit?

11. Who followed Hudson Taylor and gave the China Inland Mission its remarkable vision and direction?

12. Who discipled George Müller and snatched him as a young man from a sinful lifestyle?

13. Who were the parents of the godly and gifted prophet Daniel?

Okay, how did you do? Over fifty percent? Maybe twenty-five percent? Not quite that good?

Before you excuse your inability to answer the questions by calling the quiz "trivia," better stop and think. Had it not been for those unknown people—those "nobodies"— a huge chunk of church history would be missing. And a lot of lives would have been untouched.

Nobodies.

What a necessary band of men and women . . . servants of the King . . . yet nameless in the kingdom! Men and women who, with silent heroism, yet faithful diligence, relinquish the limelight and live in the shade of public figures.

What was it Jim Elliot, the martyred messenger of the gospel to the Aucas, once called missionaries? Something like *a bunch of nobodies trying to exalt Somebody.*

But don't mistake anonymous for *unnecessary.* Otherwise, the whole Body gets crippled . . . even paralyzed . . . or, at best, terribly dizzy as the majority of the members within the Body become diseased with self-pity and discouragement. Face it, friend, the Head of the Body calls the shots. It is His prerogative to publicize some and hide others. Don't ask me why He chooses whom He uses.

If it's His desire to use you as a Melanchthon rather than a Luther . . . or a Kimball rather than a Moody . . . or an Onesiphorus rather than a Paul . . . or a Hoste rather than a Taylor, relax!

Better than that, give God praise! You're among that elite group mentioned in 1 Corinthians 12 as:

. . . *some of the parts that seem weakest and least important are really the most necessary.* . . . *So God has put the body together in such a way that extra honor and care are given to those parts that might otherwise seem less important* (vv. 22, 24, TLB).

If it weren't for the heroic "nobodies," we wouldn't have top-notch officers to give a church its leadership. Or quality sound when everyone shows up to worship. Or janitors who clean when everyone is long gone. Or committees to provide dozens of services behind the scenes. Or mission volunteers who staff offices at home or work in obscurity overseas with only a handful of people. Come to think of it, if it weren't for the faithful "nobodies," you wouldn't even have this book in your hands right now.

Nobodies . . . exalting Somebody.

Are you one? Listen to me! It's the "nobodies" Somebody chooses so carefully. And when *He* has selected you for that role, He does not consider you a nobody.

Be encouraged!

Call for Help!

A PRAYER TO BE SAID
  WHEN THE WORLD HAS GOTTEN YOU
    DOWN,
  AND YOU FEEL ROTTEN,
  AND YOU'RE TOO DOGGONE TIRED
    TO PRAY,
  AND YOU'RE IN A BIG HURRY,
  AND BESIDES, YOU'RE MAD AT
    EVERYBODY . . .
                                    help.

There it was. One of those posters. Some are funny. Some are clever. Others beautiful. A few, thought-provoking. This one? Convicting. God really wanted me to get the message. He nudged me at a Christian conference center recently when I first read it in an administrator's office. A few weeks and many miles later He shot me the signal again—I practically ran into the same poster in a friend's office. Then just last week, while moving faster than a speeding bullet through a Portland publishing firm, I came face to face with it *again*. But this time the message broke through my defenses and wrestled me to the mat for the full count.

"My son, slow down. Ease back. Admit your needs."

Such good counsel. But so tough to carry out. Why is that? Why in the world is it such a struggle for us to cry out for assistance?

—Ants do it all the time and look at all *they* achieve.

—In my whole life I have never seen a football game won without substitutions.

—Even the finest of surgeons will arrange for help in extensive or delicate operations.

—Highway patrolmen travel in pairs.

—Through my whole career in the Marine Corps I was drilled to dig a foxhole for *two* in the event of battle.

Asking for help is smart. It's also the answer to fatigue and the "I'm indispensable" image. But something keeps us from this wise course of action, and that something is *pride.* Plain, stubborn unwillingness to admit need. The greatest battle many believers fight today is not with inefficiency, but with *super*efficiency. It's been bred into us by high-achieving parents, through years of high-pressure competition in school, and by that unyielding inner voice that keeps urging us to "Prove it to 'em! Show 'em you can do it without anyone's help!"

The result, painful though it is to admit, is a life-style of impatience. We become easily irritated—often angry. We work longer hours. Take less time off. Forget how to laugh. Cancel vacations. Allow longer and longer gaps between meaningful times in God's Word. Enjoy fewer and fewer moments in prayer and meditation. And all the while the specter of discouragement looms across our horizon like a dark storm front—threatening to choke out any remaining sunshine.

Say, my friend, it's time to declare it. You are not the Messiah of the twentieth century! There is no way you can keep pushing your life at that pace and expect to stay effective. Analyze yourself any way you please, you are H-U-M-A-N . . . nothing more. So? So slow down. So give yourself a break. So stop trying to cover all the bases and sell popcorn in the stands at the same time. So relax for a change!

Once you've put it in neutral, crack open your Bible to Exodus 18 and read aloud verses 18-27. It's the account of a visit Jethro made to the work place of his son-in-law. A fella by the name of Moses. Old Jethro frowned as he watched Moses flash from one need to another, from one person to another. From early morning until late at night the harried leader of the Israelites was neck-deep in decisions and activities. He must have looked very impressive—eating on the run, ripping from one end of camp to the other, planning appointments, meeting deadlines.

But Jethro wasn't impressed. "What is this thing that you are doing for the people?" he asked. Moses was somewhat defensive (most too-busy people are) as he attempted to justify his ridiculous schedule. Jethro didn't buy the story. Instead, he advised his son-in-law against trying to do everything alone. He reproved him with strong words:

"The thing that you are doing is not good. You will surely wear out. . . ."

The Hebrew term means "to become old, exhausted." In three words, he told Moses to

CALL FOR HELP

The benefits of shifting and sharing the load? Read verses 22-23 for yourself. "It will be easier for you . . . you will be able to endure." That's interesting, isn't it? God wants our life-style to be easier than most of us realize. We seem to think it's more commendable and "spiritual" to have that tired-blood, overworked-underpaid, I've-really-got-it-tough look. You know, the martyr complex. That strained expression that conveys "I'm working so hard for Jesus" to the public. Maybe *they're* fooled, but *He* isn't. The truth of the matter is quite the contrary. That hurried, harried appearance usually means, "I'm too stubborn to slow down" or "I'm too insecure to say 'no' " or "I'm too proud to ask for help."

Since when is a bleeding ulcer a sign of spirituality? Or no time off and a seventy-hour week a mark of efficiency? When will we learn that efficiency is enhanced not by what we accomplish but more often by what we relinquish?

The world beginning to get you down? Feeling rotten? Too tired to pray . . . in too big a hurry? Ticked off at a lot of folks? Let me suggest one of the few four-letter words God loves to hear us shout when we're angry or discouraged:

HELP!

The Hammer, the File, and the Furnace

It was the enraptured Rutherford who said in the midst of very painful trials and heartaches:

Praise God for the hammer, the file, and the furnace!

Let's think about that. The hammer is a useful and handy instrument. It is an essential and helpful tool, if nails are ever to be driven into place. Each blow forces them to bite deeper as the hammer's head pounds and pounds.

But if the nail had feelings and intelligence, it would give us another side of the story. To the nail, the hammer is a brutal, relentless master—an enemy who loves to beat it into submission. That is the nail's view of the hammer. It is correct. Except for one thing. The nail tends to forget that both it and the hammer are held by the same workman. The workman decides whose "head" will be pounded out of sight . . . and which hammer will be used to do the job.

This decision is the sovereign right of the carpenter. Let the nail but remember that it and the hammer are held by the same workman . . . and its resentment will fade as it yields to the carpenter without complaint.

The same analogy holds true for the metal that endures the rasp of the file and the blast of the furnace. If the metal forgets that it and the tools are objects of the same craftsman's care, it will build up hatred and resentment. The metal must keep in mind that the craftsman knows what he's doing . . . and is doing what is best.

Heartaches and disappointments are like the hammer, the file, and the furnace. They come in all shapes and sizes: an unfulfilled romance, a lingering illness, an untimely death, an unachieved goal in life, a broken home or marriage, a severed friendship, a wayward and rebellious child, a personal medical report that advises "immediate surgery," a failing grade at school, a depression that simply won't go away, a habit you can't seem to break. Sometimes heartaches come suddenly . . . other times they appear over the passing of many months, slowly as the erosion of earth.

Do I write to a "nail" that has begun to resent the blows of the hammer? Are you at the brink of despair, thinking that you cannot bear another day of heartache? Is that what's gotten you down?

As difficult as it may be for you to believe this today, the Master knows what He's doing. Your Savior knows your breaking point. The bruising and crushing and melting process is designed to reshape you, *not ruin you.* Your value is increasing the longer He lingers over you.

A. W. Tozer agrees:

It is doubtful whether God can bless a man greatly until He has hurt him deeply.

Aching friend—stand fast. Like David when calamity caved in, strengthen yourself in the Lord your God (1 Samuel 30:6). God's hand is in your heartache. Yes, it is!

If you weren't important, do you think He would take this long and work this hard on your life? Those whom God uses most effectively have been hammered, filed, and tempered in the furnace of trials and heartache.

An Antidote for Weariness

It was about twenty years ago that my brother, now on the mission field, introduced a hymn to me I'd not heard before. He loves to play the piano—and plays it beautifully—so he sat at the keyboard and played the simple melody and sang the beloved words of a hymn I have since committed to memory.

The melodic strains of this piece often accompany me as I drive or take a walk in solitude or return late from a day of pressure and demands. Actually the hymn is not new; it's an old piece based on an early Greek hymn that dates as far back as the eighth century.

> Art thou weary, art thou languid,
>   Art thou sore distressed?
> "Come to me," saith One, "And coming
>   Be at rest."
> Hath He marks to lead me to Him
>   If He be my Guide?
> In His feet and hands are wound-prints,
>   And His side.
> Finding, following, keeping, struggling,
>   Is He sure to bless?
> Saints, apostles, prophets, martyrs,
>   Answer, "Yes."[6]

Surely in the home and heart of some soul who reads this book, there is a silent sigh, a twinge of spiritual fatigue . . . a deep and abiding weariness. It's no wonder! Our pace, the incessant activity, the noise, the interruptions, the deadlines and demands, the daily schedule, and the periodic feelings of failure and futility bombard our beings like the shelling of a beachhead. Our natural tendency is to wave a white flag, shouting, "I give up! I surrender!" This, of course, is the dangerous extreme of being weary—the decision to bail out, to throw in the towel, to give in to discouragement and give up. There is nothing wrong or unnatural with feeling weary, but there is everything wrong with abandoning ship in the midst of the fight.

Growing weary is the consequence of many experiences—none of them bad, but all of them exhausting. To name just a few:

We can be weary of *waiting.* *"I am weary with my crying; my throat is parched; my eyes fail while I wait for my God"* (Psalm 69:3 NASV).

We can be weary of *studying and learning. "Of making many books there is no end, and much study wearies the body"* (Ecclesiastes 12:12).

We can be weary of *fighting the enemy. "He arose and struck the Philistines until his hand was weary and clung to the sword"* (2 Samuel 23:10 NASV).

We can be weary of *criticism and persecution.*

I am weary with my sighing;
Every night I make my bed swim,
I dissolve my couch with my tears.
My eye has wasted away with grief;
It has become old because of all my adversaries
(Psalm 6:6-7 NASV).

Lots of things are fine in themselves, but our strength has its limits . . . and before long fatigue cuts our feet out from beneath us. The longer the weariness lingers, the more we face the danger of that weary condition clutching our inner man by the throat and strangling our hope, our motivation, our spark, our optimism, our encouragement.

Like Isaiah, I want to "sustain the weary" with a word of

encouragement (Isaiah 50:4). Since our Lord never grows weary, He is able to give strength to the weary—He really is! If you question that, you *must* stop and read Isaiah 40:28-31. Do that right now.

But let's understand that God does not dispense strength and encouragement like a druggist fills your prescription. The Lord doesn't promise to give us something to *take* so we can handle our weary moments. He promises us *Himself.* That is all. And that is enough.

The Savior says:

"Come to me, all you who are weary and burdened, and I will give you rest. Take my yoke upon you and learn from me, for I am gentle and humble in heart, and you will find rest for your souls. For my yoke is easy and my burden is light" (Matthew 11:28-30).

And Paul writes:

For he himself is our peace . . . (Ephesians 2:14).

In place of our exhaustion and spiritual fatigue, He will give us rest. All He asks is that we come to Him . . . that we spend a while thinking about Him, meditating on Him, talking to Him, listening in silence, occupying ourselves with Him—totally and thoroughly lost in the hiding place of His presence.

Consider him . . . so that you will not grow weary and lose heart (Hebrews 12:3).

Growing weary, please observe, can result in losing heart.

Art thou weary? Heavy laden? Distressed? Come to the Savior. Come immediately, come repeatedly, come boldly. And be at rest.

When was the last time you came to the Lord, all alone, and gave Him your load of care?

No wonder you're discouraged. You're weary!

Come. Unload. He can handle it.

"Final Descent . . ." Commence Prayer"

The following incident took place in 1968 on an air-liner bound for New York. It was a routine flight, and normally a boring affair. The kind of flights I like—uneventful. But this one proved to be otherwise.

Descending to the destination, the pilot realized the landing gear refused to engage. He worked the controls back and forth, trying again and again to make the gear lock down into place. No success. He then asked the control tower for instructions as he circled the landing field. Responding to the crisis, airport personnel sprayed the runway with foam as fire trucks and other emergency vehicles moved into position. Disaster was only minutes away.

The passengers, meanwhile, were told of each maneuver in that calm, cheery voice pilots manage to use at times like this. Flight attendants glided about the cabin with an air of cool reserve. Passengers were told to place their heads between their knees and grab their ankles just before impact. It was one of those I-can't-believe-this-is-happening-to-me experiences. There were tears, no doubt, and a few screams of despair. The landing was now seconds away.

Suddenly the pilot announced over the intercom:

We are beginning our final descent. At this moment, in ac-cordance with International Aviation Codes established at Geneva, it is my obligation to inform you that if you believe in God you should commence prayer.

I'm happy to report that the belly landing occurred without a hitch. No one was injured and, aside from some rather extensive damage to the plane, the airline hardly remembered the incident. In fact, a relative of one of the passengers called the airline the very next day and asked about the prayer rule the pilot had quoted. No one volunteered any information on the subject. Back to that cool reserve, it was simply, "No comment."

Amazing. The only thing that brought out into the open a deep-down "secret rule" was crisis. Pushed to the brink, back to the wall, right up to the wire, all escape routes closed . . . only then does our society crack open a hint of recognition that God just might be there and—"if you believe . . . you should commence prayer."

Reminds me of a dialogue I watched on the tube the other night. The guy being interviewed had "come back alive" from Mount St. Helens with pictures *and sound track* of his own personal nightmare. A reporter for a local television station, he was in close proximity to the crater when the mountain suddenly rumbled to life, spewing steam and ash miles into the air. The reporter literally ran for his life. With camera rolling and the mike on. The pictures were, of course, blurred and murky, but his voice was something else. Periodically, he'd click on his gear.

He admitted after all this was played on the talk show that he only vaguely recalled saying many of those things. It was eerie, almost too personal to be disclosed. He breathed deeply, sobbed several times, panted, and spoke directly to God. No formality, no clichés—just the despairing cry of a creature in a crisis. Things like, "Oh, God, oh, my God . . . help! Help!! . . . Oh, Lord God, get me through. God, I need you, please help me; I don't know where I am"—more sobbing, more rapid breathing, spitting, gagging, coughing, panting—"It's so hot, so dark, help me, God! Please, please, please, please . . . oh, God!"

There's nothing to compare with crisis when it comes

to finding out the otherwise hidden truth of the soul. Any soul. We may mask it, ignore it, pass it off with cool sophistication and intellectual denial . . . but take away the cushion of comfort, remove the shield of safety, interject the threat of death without the presence of people to take the panic out of the moment, and it's fairly certain most in the ranks of humanity "commence prayer."

David certainly did. When in "the slimy pit . . . the mud and mire," he testifies that Jehovah heard his cry (Psalm 40:1-2). So did Paul and Silas in that ancient Philippian prison when all seemed hopeless (Acts 16:25-26). It was from "the deep" Jonah cried for help . . . choking on salt water and engulfed by the Mediterranean currents, the prodigal prophet called out in his distress (Jonah 2:1-4). Old King Nebuchadnezzar did, too, fresh off a siege of insanity when he had lost his reason and lived like a wild beast in the open field. That former mental patient "raised his eyes toward heaven" and poured out the feelings of his soul to the Lord God, the very One the king had denied in earlier years (Daniel 4:29-37).

Crisis crushes. And in crushing, it often refines and purifies. You may be discouraged today because the crushing has not yet led to a surrender. I've stood beside too many of the dying, ministered to too many of the broken and bruised to believe that crushing is an end in itself. Unfortunately, however, it usually takes the brutal blows of affliction to soften and penetrate hard hearts. Even though such blows often seem unfair.

Remember Alexander Solzhenitsyn's admission:

It was only when I lay there on rotting prison straw that I sensed within myself the first stirrings of good. Gradually, it was disclosed to me that the line separating good and evil passes, not through states, nor between classes, nor between political parties either, but right through all human hearts. So, bless you, prison, for having been in my life.[5]

Those words provide a perfect illustration of the psalmist's instruction:

Before I was afflicted I went astray,
but now I obey your word.
It was good for me to be afflicted
so that I might learn your decrees (Psalm 119:67, 71).

After crises crush sufficiently, God steps in to comfort and teach.

Feel headed for a crash? Engulfed in crisis? Tune in the calm voice of your Pilot.

He knows precisely what He is doing. And belly-landings don't frighten Him one bit.

Part Two:

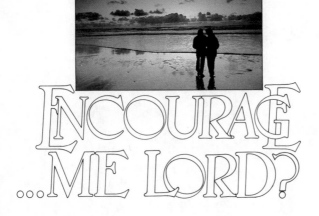

ENCOURAGE
...ME LORD?

"One of the highest of human duties is the duty of encouragement. . . . It is easy to laugh at men's ideals; it is easy to pour cold water on their enthusiasm; it is easy to discourage others. The world is full of discouragers. We have a Christian duty to encourage one another. Many a time a word of praise or thanks or appreciation or cheer has kept a man on his feet. Blessed is the man who speaks such a word."[7]

—William Barclay

Now if your experience of
Christ's encouragement and love
means anything to you, if you have
known something of the fellowship
of his Spirit, and all that it means
in kindness and deep sympathy, do
make my best hopes for you come
true! Live together in love, as
though you had only one mind and
one spirit between you. Never act
from motives of rivalry or personal
vanity, but in humility think more
of one another than you do of
yourselves. None of you should
think only of his own affairs, but
each should learn to see things
from other people's point of view.
Let Christ Jesus be your example
as to what your attitude should be.

(Philippians 2:1-5 Phillips)

Take Time to Be Tender

Back when I was a kid I got a bellyache that wouldn't go away. It hurt so bad I couldn't stand up straight. Or sit down without increasing the pain. Finally, my folks hauled me over to a big house in West Houston where a doctor lived. He had turned the back section into his office and clinic.

It was a hot, muggy afternoon. I was scared.

The doc decided I needed a quick exam—but he really felt I was suffering from an attack of appendicitis. He had whispered that with certainty under his breath to my mom. I remember the fear that gripped me when I pictured myself having to go to a big, white-brick hospital, be put to sleep, get cut on, then endure having those stitches jerked out.

Looking back, however, I really believe that "quick exam" hurt worse than surgery the next day. The guy was rough, I mean really rough. He poked and thumped and pulled and pushed at me like I was Raggedy Andy. I was already in pain, but when old Dr. Vice Grip got through, I felt like I had been his personal punching bag. To him, I was nothing more than a ten-year-old specimen of humanity. Male, blond, slight build, ninety-nine-degree temperature, with undetermined abdominal pain—and nauseated.

Never once do I recall his looking at me, listening to me, talking with me, or encouraging me in any way. Although young, I distinctly remember feeling like I bored the man—like case No. 13 that day, appendectomy No. 796 for him in his practice. And if the truth were known, an irritating interruption in his plans for nine holes later that afternoon.

Granted, a ten-year-old with a bellyache is not the greatest challenge for a seasoned physician to face . . . but his insensitivity left a lasting impression. His lack of tender caring canceled out the significance of all those neatly framed diplomas, achievements, and awards plastered across the wall behind his desk. He may have been bright . . . but he was even *more* brutal.

At that painful, terrifying moment of my life, I needed more than credentials. Even as a little kid I needed compassion. A touch of kindness. A gentle, considerate, soft-spoken word of assurance. Something to cushion the blows of the man's cut-and-dried verdict, "This boy needs surgery—meet me at Memorial at five o'clock today." Over and out.

Looking back over thirty-five years, I've learned a valuable lesson: When people are hurting, they need more than an accurate analysis and diagnosis. More than professional advice. More, much more, than a stern, firm turn of a verbal wrench that cinches everything down tight.

Attorneys, doctors, counselors, physical therapists, dentists, fellow ministers, nurses, teachers, disciplers, parents, hear ye, *hear ye!* Fragile and delicate are the feelings of most who seek our help. They need to sense we are there because we care . . . not just because it's our job. Truth and tact make great bedfellows.

Sound too liberal? Weak? Would it help if you could see that someone like the Apostle Paul embraced this philosophy? He did. Although a brilliant and disciplined man, he was tender.

You know we never used flattery, nor did we put on a mask to cover up greed—God is our witness. We were not looking for praise from men, not from you or anyone else.

As apostles of Christ we could have been a burden to you, but we were gentle among you, like a mother caring for her little children. We loved you so much that we were delighted to share with you not only the gospel of God but our lives as well, because you had become so dear to us" (1 Thessalonians 2:5-8).

Someday we shall all be at the receiving end—you can count on it. We shall be the ones in need of affirmation, encouragement, a gentle touch of tenderness. It's like the time-worn counsel of the good doctor Thomas Sydenham, the "English Hippocrates" (1624-1689). Addressing himself to the professionals of his day, Dr. Sydenham wrote:

> *It becomes every person who purposes to give himself to the care of others, seriously to consider the four following things: First, that he must one day give an account to the Supreme judge of all the lives entrusted to his care. Second, that all his skill and knowledge and energy, as they have been given him by God, so they should be exercised for His glory and the good of mankind, and not for mere gain or ambition. Third, and not more beautifully than truly, let him reflect that he has undertaken the care of no mean creature; for, in order that he may estimate the value, the greatness of the human race, the only begotten Son of God became himself a man, and thus ennobled it with His divine dignity, and far more than this, died to redeem it. And fourth, that the doctor being himself a mortal human being, should be diligent and tender in relieving his suffering patients, inasmuch as he himself must one day be a like sufferer.*[8]

And that applies to ten-year-olds with a bellyache, eighty-year-olds with a backache, anybody with a headache . . . and everybody with a heartache.

A Bridge Called Credibility

March 11, 1942, was a dark, desperate day at Corregidor. The Pacific theater of war was threatening and bleak. One island after another had been buffeted into submission. The enemy was now marching into the Philippines as confident and methodical as the star band in the Rose Bowl parade. Surrender was inevitable. The brilliant and bold soldier, Douglas MacArthur, had only three words for his comrades as he stepped into the escape boat destined for Australia:

I SHALL RETURN.

Upon arriving nine days later in the port of Adelaide, the sixty-two-year-old military statesman closed his remarks with this sentence:

I CAME THROUGH AND I SHALL RETURN.

A little over 2½ years later—October 20, 1944, to be exact—he stood once again on Philippine soil after landing safely at Leyte Island. This is what he said:

This is the voice of freedom, General MacArthur speaking. People of the Philippines: I HAVE RETURNED!

MacArthur kept his word. His word was as good as his bond. Regardless of the odds against him, including the pressures and power of enemy strategy, he was bound and determined to make his promise good.

This rare breed of man is almost extinct. Whether an executive or an apprentice, a student or a teacher, a blue collar or white, a Christian or pagan—rare indeed are those who keep their word. The prevalence of the problem has caused the coining of terms painfully familiar to us in our era: *credibility gap*. To say that something is "credible" is to say it is "capable of being believed, trustworthy." To refer to a "gap" in such suggests a "breach or a reason for doubt."

Jurors often have reason to doubt the testimony of a witness on the stand. Parents, likewise, have reason at times to doubt their children's word (and vice versa). Citizens frequently doubt the promises of politicians and the credibility of an employee's word is questioned by the employer. Creditors can no longer believe a debtor's verbal promise to pay and many a mate has ample reason to doubt the word of his or her partner. This is a terrible dilemma! Precious few do what they *say* they will do without a reminder, a warning, or a threat. Unfortunately, this is true even among Christians.

Listen to what the Scriptures have to say about keeping your word:

> *Therefore each of you must put off falsehood and speak truthfully to his neighbor . . .* (Ephesians 4:25).

> *And whatever you do, whether in word or deed, do it all in the name of the Lord Jesus . . .* (Colossians 3:17).

> *O LORD, who may abide in Thy tent?*
> *Who may dwell on Thy holy hill?*
> *He who walks with integrity . . .*
> *And speaks truth in his heart* (Psalm 15:1-2 NASV).

> *It is better not to vow than to make a vow and not fulfill it* (Ecclesiastes 5:5).

> *When a man . . . takes an oath to obligate himself by a pledge, he must not break his word but must do everything he said* (Numbers 30:2).

Question: Judging yourself on this matter of keeping your word, are you bridging or widening the credibility gap? Are you encouraging or discouraging others? Let me help you answer that by using four familiar situations.

1. When you reply, "Yes, I'll pray for you"—do you?

2. When you tell someone they can depend on you to help them out—can they?

3. When you say you'll be there at such-and-such a time—are you?

4. When you obligate yourself to pay a debt on time—do you?

Granted, no one's perfect. But if you fail, do you own up to it? Do you quickly admit your failure to the person you promised and refuse to rationalize around it? If you do you are *really* rare . . . but a person of genuine integrity. And one who is an encouragement and can encourage others.

Do you know something? I know another One who promised He would return. He, too, will keep His word. In fact, He's never broken one promise. There's no credibility gap with Him. He *will* return. I can hardly wait to see His smiling face.

Talk about encouragement!

Stay in Circulation

People who encourage people aren't loners, out of touch with humanity, distant and unreachable.

During the reign of Oliver Cromwell, the British government began to run low on silver for coins. Lord Cromwell sent his men on an investigation of the local cathedral to see if they could find any precious metal there. After investigating, they reported:

> The only silver we could find is in the statues of the saints standing in the corners.

To which the radical soldier and statesman of England replied:

> Good! We'll melt down the saints and put them into circulation![9]

Not bad theology for a proper, strait-laced, Lord Protector of the Isles, huh? In a few words the direct order states the essence . . . the kernel . . . the practical goal of authentic Christianity. Not rows of silver saints, highly polished, frequently dusted, crammed into the corners of elegant cathedrals. Not plaster people cloaked in thin layers of untarnished silver and topped with a metallic halo. But *real* persons. Melted saints circulating through the mainstream of humanity. Bringing worth and value down where life transpires in the raw. Without the faint aura of stained glass, the electric modulation of the organ, and the familiar comforts of padded pews and dimmed lights. Out where bottom-line theology is top-shelf priority. You know the places:

☐   On campuses where students scrape through the varnish of shallow answers.

☐   In the shop where unbelieving employees test the mettle of everyday Christianity.

☐   At home with a houseful of kids, where "R and R" means Run and Rassle.

☐   In the concrete battlegrounds of sales competition, seasonal conventions, and sexual temptations, where hard-core assaults are made on internal character.

☐   On the hospital bed, when reality never takes a nap.

☐   In the office, where diligence and honesty are forever on the scaffold.

☐   On the team where patience and self-control are X-rayed under pressure.

It's easy to kid ourselves. So easy. The Christian must guard against self-deception. We can begin to consider ourselves martyrs because we are in church twice on Sunday—really sacrificing by investing a few hours on the "day of rest." Listen, my friend, being among the saints is no sacrifice . . . it's a brief, choice privilege. The cost factor occurs on Monday or Tuesday . . . and during the rest of the week. That's when we're "melted down and put into circulation." That's when they go for the jugular. And it is remarkable how that monotonous work-week test discolors many a silver saint. "Sunday religion" may seem sufficient, but it isn't. Deception can easily result in a surprise ending.

> *Shed a tear for Jimmy Brown*
>   *Poor Jimmy is no more.*
> *For what he thought was H_2O*
>   *Was H_2SO_4.*

It's the acid grind that takes the toll, isn't it? Maybe that explains why the venerable prophet of God touched a nerve with his probing query:

If racing with mere men—these men of Anathoth—has wearied you, how will you race against horses, . . . If you stumble and fall on open ground, what will you do in Jordan's jungles? (Jeremiah 12:5, TLB).

Doing battle in the steaming jungle calls for shock troops in super shape. No rhinestone cowboys can cut it among the swamps and insects of the gross world system. Sunday-go-to-meetin' silver saints in shining armor are simply out of circulation if that's the limit to their faith. Waging wilderness warfare calls for sweat . . . energy . . . keen strategy . . . determination . . . a good supply of ammunition . . . willingness to fight . . . refusal to surrender, even with the elephants tromping on your airhose.

And *that* is why we must be melted! It's all part of being "in circulation." Those who successfully wage war with silent heroism under relentless secular pressure—ah, *they* are the saints who know what it means to be melted.

You can opt for an easier path. Sure. You can keep your own record and come out smelling like a rose. Your game plan might look something like this:

Dressed up and drove to church.	Check
Walked three blocks in the rain.	Check
Got a seat and sat quietly.	Check
Sang each verse, smiled appropriately.	Check
Gave $5 . . . listened to the sermon.	Check
Closed my Bible, prayed, looked pious.	Check
Shook hands . . . walked out, quickly forgot.	Check

Still a saint? Uh-huh . . . a silver one, in fact. Polished to a high-gloss sheen. Icily regular, cool and casual, consistently present . . . and safely out of circulation. Another touch-me-not whatnot.

. . . until the Lord calls for an investigation of the local cathedral.

The Fine Art of Blowing It

It happens to every one of us. Teachers as well as students. Cops as well as criminals. Bosses as well as secretaries. Parents as well as kids. The diligent as well as the lazy. Not even presidents are immune. Or corporation heads who earn six-figure salaries. The same is true of well-meaning architects and hard-working builders and clear-thinking engineers . . . not to mention pro ball players, politicians, and preachers.

What? Making mistakes, that's what. Doing the wrong thing, usually with the best of motives. And it happens with remarkable regularity.

Let's face it, success is overrated. All of us crave it despite daily proof that man's real genius lies in quite the opposite direction. It's really incompetence that we're all pros at. Which brings me to a basic question that has been burning inside me for months: How come we're so surprised when we see it in others and so devastated when it has occurred in ourselves?

Show me the guy who wrote the rules for perfectionism and I'll guarantee he's a nailbiter with a face full of tics . . . whose wife dreads to see him come home. Furthermore, he forfeits the right to be respected because he's either guilty of not admitting he blew it or he has become an expert at cover-up.

You can do that, you know. Stop and think of ways certain people can keep from coming out and confessing they

blew it. Doctors can bury their mistakes. Lawyers' mistakes get shut up in prison—literally. Dentists' mistakes
are pulled. Plumbers' mistakes are stopped. Carpenters
turn theirs into sawdust. I like what I read in a magazine
recently.

> Just in case you find any mistakes in this magazine, please
> remember they were put there for a purpose. We try to offer
> something for everyone. Some people are always looking for
> mistakes and we didn't want to disappoint you!

Hey, there have been some real winners! Back in 1957,
Ford bragged about "the car of the decade." The Edsel.
Unless you lucked out, the Edsel you bought had a door
that wouldn't close, a hood that wouldn't open, a horn
that kept getting stuck, paint that peeled, and a transmis-
sion that wouldn't fulfill its mission. One business writer
likened the Edsel's sales graph to an extremely dangerous
ski slope. He added that so far as he knew, there was only
one case on record of an Edsel ever being stolen.

And how about that famous tower in Italy? The "leaning tower," almost twenty feet out of perpendicular. The
guy that planned that foundation to be only ten feet deep
(for a building 179 feet tall) didn't possess the world's
largest brain. How would you like to have listed in your re-
sumé, "Designed the Leaning Tower of Pisa"?

A friend of mine, realizing how adept I am in this business of blowing it, passed on to me an amazing book (accurate, but funny) entitled *The Incomplete Book of Failures* by
Stephen Pile. Appropriately, the book itself had two missing pages when it was printed, so the first thing you read is
an apology for the omission—and an erratum slip that
provides the two pages.

Among the many wild and crazy reports are such things
as the least successful weather report, the worst computer,
the most boring lecture, the worst aircraft, the slowest
selling book, the smallest ever audience, the ugliest building ever constructed, the most chaotic wedding cere-

mony, and some of the worst statements . . . proven wrong by posterity. Some of those statements, for example, were:

> *"Far too noisy, my dear Mozart. Far too many notes."*
> —The Emperor Ferdinand after the first performance of *The Marriage of Figaro.*

> *"If Beethoven's Seventh Symphony is not by some means abridged, it will soon fall into disuse."*
> —Philip Hale, Boston music critic, 1837

> *"Rembrandt is not to be compared in the painting of character with our extraordinarily gifted English artist Mr. Rippingille."*
> —John Hunt (1775-1848)

> *"Flight by machines heavier than air is unpractical and insignificant . . . utterly impossible."*
> —Simon Newcomb (1835-1909)

> *"We don't like their sound. Groups of guitars are on their way out."*
> —Decca Recording Company when turning down the Beatles in 1962.

> *"You will never amount to very much."*
> —A Munich schoolmaster to Albert Einstein, aged 10.[10]

And on and on it goes. The only thing we can be thankful for when it comes to blowing it is that nobody keeps a record of ours. Or do they? Or do you with *others?* Not if you are serious about encouragement.

Come on, ease off. If our perfect Lord is gracious enough to take our worst, our ugliest, our most boring, our least successful, our leaning-tower failures, our Edsel flops, and forgive them, burying them in the depths of the sea, then it's high time we give each other a break.

In fact, He promises full acceptance along with full forgiveness in print for all to read . . . without an erratum sheet attached. Isn't that encouraging? Can't we be that type of encourager to one another? After all, imperfection is one of the few things we still have in common. It links us close together in the same family!

So then, whenever one of us blows it and we can't hide it, how about a little support from those who haven't been caught yet?

Oops, correction. How about a *lot* of support?

The Heart of Encouragement

The heart of the word "cordial" is the word "heart." The heart of "heart" is *kardia*, a Greek term that most often refers to the center of a person's inner life . . . the source or seat of all the forces and functions of our inner being. So when we think about being cordial, we are thinking about something that comes from and affects the very center of life itself. Maybe that's why the dictionary defines "cordial" like this:

> . . . *of or relating to the heart: vital, tending to revive, cheer or invigorate, heartfelt, gracious.* . . .

That's really a mouthful (or a heartful). In fact, that's worth a few minutes' meditation.

Being cordial literally starts from the heart, as I see it. Its origin begins with the deep-seated belief that the other guy is important, genuinely significant, deserving of my undivided attention and my unrivaled interest, if only for a few seconds. As cordiality is encouraged by such a belief, it then prompts me to be sensitive to that person's feelings.

If a person is uneasy and self-conscious, cordiality alerts me to put him at ease, to help him feel comfortable. If he is shy, cordiality provides a relief. If he is bored and bothered, cordiality stimulates and invigorates him. If he is sad and gloomy, cordiality brings cheer; it revives and rejuvenates him. What a needed and necessary virtue it is!

How do we project cordiality? In answer to that question, I suggest at least four basic ingredients:

1. A warm smile

Now lest you try, let me warn you against faking this. You don't learn to smile by practicing in front of a mirror. A smile has to be a natural part of your whole person, reflecting a friendliness that is genuine. There is nothing about you more magnetic or attractive than your smile. It will fit most every occasion, and it will communicate volumes to the other person.

When a king's face brightens, it means life;
his favor is like a rain cloud in spring (Proverbs 16:15).

I'm afraid that some long-faced saints would crack their concrete masks if they smiled—I really am! Nothing repels like a frown . . . or attracts like a smile. It's downright contagious.

2. A solid handshake

Now I'm something of a specialist when it comes to handshakes. I've experienced about every kind.

Some are bonebreakers—like a cross between King Kong and Goliath (sometimes even from little, elderly ladies!). Others are completely boneless—like a handful of cool seaweed or a glove full of warm pudding. Some handshakes leave you exhausted, some cling like a crab, others turn into a small; curious wrestling match, never wanting to let go.

There are those, however, that are solid, sure, filled with such thoughts as, "Oh, how I appreciate you!" and "My, it's good to be in your presence!" and "Let me assure you of my love and interest!" Those say, "You're terrific!"

Never underestimate the value of this cordial expression. The handshake is one of a rare remaining species threatened with extinction in the family of touch. This is one of the quiet ways you "sharpen the iron" of another with your "iron" (Proverbs 27:17).

3. Direct eye contact

Accompanying every handshake and conversation, no

matter how brief, ought to be an eyeball-to-eyeball encounter. The eyes reflect deep feelings enclosed in the secret chamber of your soul, which have no other means of release. This allows others to read how you feel about them. Cordiality cannot be expressed indirectly.

4. A word of encouragement

Keep this fresh, free from clichés, and to the point. Call his name (or ask for it) and use it as you talk. If time permits, mention something you honestly appreciate about him. Be specific and natural, but do not try to flatter the person. Let your heart be freely felt as your words flow.

Oil and perfume make the heart glad,
So a man's counsel is sweet to his friend
(Proverbs 27:9 NASV).

People who encourage are cordial. Are you?

Dress Your Dreams in Denim

Some collegians think manual labor is the president of Mexico . . . until they graduate. Suddenly, the light dawns. Reality frowns. And that sheltered, brainy, fair-skinned, squint-eyed scholar who has majored in medieval literature and minored in Latin comes of age. He experiences a strange sensation deep within his abdomen two weeks after framing his diploma. Hunger. Remarkable motivation accompanies this feeling.

His attempts at finding employment prove futile. Those places that have an opening don't really need a guy with a master's in medieval lit. They can't even spell it. Who cares if a truck driver understands European poetry from the twelfth century? Or what does it matter if the fella stocking the shelves at Safeway can give you the ninth letter in the Latin alphabet? When it comes to landing a job, most employers are notoriously pragmatic and unsophisticated. They are looking for people who have more than academic, gray wrinkles between their ears. They really couldn't care less about how much a guy or gal knows. What they want is someone who can *put to use* the knowledge that's been gained, whether the field is geology or accounting, engineering or plumbing, physics or barbering, journalism or welding.

That doesn't just happen. People who are in great demand today are those who can see it in their imaginations—then pull it off. Those who can think—then follow through. Those who dress their daring dreams in practical denim workclothes. That takes a measure of gift, a pinch of skill, and a ton of discipline! Being practical requires that we traffic in reality, staying flexible at the intersections where stop-and-go lights flash. It also demands an understanding of others who are driving so as to avoid collisions.

Another mark of practicality is a constant awareness of time. The life of a practical person is fairly uncomplicated and usually methodical. The practical mind would rather meet a deadline and settle for limited objectives than accomplish the maximum and be late.

The favorite expressions of a practical soul often begin with "what?"

What does the job require?

What do you expect of me?

What is the deadline?

What are the techniques?

Or "how" . . .

How does it work?

How long will it take?

How much does it cost?

How fast can it go?

Dreamers don't mix too well with pragmatists. They irritate each other when they rub together . . . yet both are necessary. Take away the former and you've got a predictable and occasionally dull result. Remove the latter and you've got creative ideas without wheels, slick visions without handles . . . and you go broke trying to get it off the runway.

The Bible is full of men and women who dreamed dreams and saw visions. But they didn't stop there. They had faith, they were people who saw the impossible, and yet their feet were planted on planet earth.

Take Nehemiah. What a man! He had the task of rebuilding the stone wall around Jerusalem. He spent days thinking, praying, observing, dreaming, and planning.

But was he ever practical! He organized a mob into work parties . . . he faced criticism realistically . . . he stayed at the task without putting out needless fires . . . he met deadlines . . . and he maintained the budget.

Or take Abigail. What a woman! She was married to a first-class fink, Nabal by name, alias Archie Bunker. Because of his lack of wisdom, his greed, prejudice, and selfishness, he aroused the ire of his employees. They laid plans to kill him. Being a woman of faith, Abigail thought through the plot, prayed, and planned. Then she did a remarkable thing. She catered a meal to those hungry, angry men. Smart gal! Because of her practicality, Nabal's life was saved and an angry band of men was calmed and turned back.

It is the practical person, writes Emerson, who becomes "a vein in times of terror that commands the admiration of the wisest." So true. Amazing thing about the practical person—he may not have the most fun or think the deepest thoughts, but he seldom goes hungry!

Just now finishing school? Looking for a job? Is this the reason you're discouraged? Remember this—dreams are great and visions are fun. But in the final analysis, when the bills come due, they'll be paid by manual labor. *Labor* . . . hard work forged in the furnace of practicality.

I encourage you . . . get with it. Be practical, that is.

"The Opra Ain't Over"

The words were painted in bright red on a banner hung over the wall near the forty-yard line of Texas Stadium, home of the Dallas Cowboys football team, on Sunday afternoon.

The guys in silver and blue were struggling to stay in the race for the playoffs. So a dyed-in-the-wool Cowboy fan decided he would offer some back-home encouragement straight out of his country-western repertoire. He scratched around his garage on Saturday and found some paint, a big brush, and a ruler . . . then splashed those words on a king-size bed sheet for all America to read:

THE OPRA AIN'T OVER
'TIL THE FAT LADY SINGS.

It was his way of saying, "We're hangin' in there, baby. Don't count us out. We have three games left before anybody can say for sure . . . so we're not givin' up! The opra ain't over."

Sure is easy to jump to conclusions, isn't it? People who study trends make it their business to manufacture out of their imaginations the proposed (and "inevitable") end result. Pollsters do that, too. After a sampling of three percent of our country, vast and stunning stats are predicted. Our worry increases. We are all informed that so-and-so will, *for sure,* wind up doing such-and-such. At times it's downright scary. And discouraging.

Every once in awhile it's helpful to remember times

when those folks wound up with egg on their faces. Much to our amazement, the incredible often happens.

- [ ] Like when Wellington whipped Napoleon
- [ ] Or Truman beat Dewey
- [ ] And Washington won in the Rose Bowl
- [ ] Like that time the earthquake didn't hit
- [ ] And England *didn't* surrender
- [ ] And Star Wars *didn't* grab a fistful of Academy Awards
- [ ] And Hitler *wasn't* the anti-Christ
- [ ] And the communists *didn't* take over America by 1980
- [ ] And Muhammad Ali *could* get beaten
- [ ] And a nation *could* continue on through the disillusionments of Viet Nam, White House and senatorial scandals, assassination attempts, energy crises, and nuclear mishaps.

Yes, at many a turn we have all been tempted to jump to so-called "obvious" conclusions, only to be surprised by a strange curve thrown our way. God is good at that. When He does, it really encourages His people.

Can you recall a few biblical examples?

- [ ] A wiry teenager, armed with only a sling and a stone, whipped a giant over nine feet tall. Nobody would've predicted that.
- [ ] With an Egyptian army fast approaching and no possible way to escape, all looked bleak. But not so! Against nature and reversing the pull of gravity, a sea opened up and allowed the Hebrews to walk across.
- [ ] And how about the vast, "indestructible" wall around Jericho? Who would've ever imagined?
- [ ] Or that dead-end street at Golgotha miraculously opening back up at an empty tomb three days later?
- [ ] Or a handful of very human disciples turning the world upside down? Anybody—and I mean anybody—who would have been near enough to have witnessed any one of those predicaments would certainly have said,

"Curtains . . . the opra is over!"

A lot of you who read this page are backed up against a set of circumstances that seem to spell T-H-E E-N-D. All looks almost hopeless. Pretty well finished. Apparently over. Maybe you need to read that again, underlining those words:

seem to . . . almost . . . pretty well . . . apparently.

Your adversary would love for you to assume the worst. He'd enjoy seeing you heave a sigh and resign yourself to depressed feelings that accompany defeat, failure, maximum resentment, and minimum faith. After all, it's fairly obvious you're through. Well . . . since when does "fairly obvious" draw the curtain on the last act? It's been my experience that when God is involved, *anything* can happen. The One who directed that stone in between Goliath's eyes and split the Red Sea down the middle and leveled that wall around Jericho and brought His Son back from beyond takes delight in mixing up the odds as He alters the obvious and bypasses the inevitable.

The blind songwriter, Fanny Crosby, put it another way:

Chords that were broken will vibrate once more. [11]

In other words, don't manufacture conclusions. Don't even think in terms of "this is the way things will turn out." Be open. Stay that way. God has a beautiful way of bringing good vibes out of broken chords. When the Lord is in it, anything is possible. In His performances there are dozens of "fat ladies" waiting to sing the finale.

The opra ain't over.

Be an Encourager!

It all comes down to this: A strong commitment to the encouragement of others. But Henry Drummond's remark haunts me at times:

> How many prodigals are kept out of the kingdom of God by the unlovely characters of those who profess to be inside!

Will you allow me, in this closing, private chat with you, to pick out one "unlovely" characteristic frequently found in Christian circles . . . and develop it from a positive point of view? I'm thinking of the *lack of encouragement* in our relationship with others. It's almost an epidemic!

To illustrate this point, when did *you* last encourage someone else? I firmly believe that an individual is never more Christ-like than when full of compassion for those who are down, needy, discouraged, or forgotten. How terribly essential is our commitment to encouragement!

Woven into the fabric of the book of Acts is the quiet yet penetrating life of a man who is a stranger to most Christians. Barnabas emerged from the island of Cyprus, destined to an abstruse role of "minister of encouragement." In fact, his name means "Son of Encouragement" according to Acts 4:36. In comparison to the brilliant spotlights of this book—Peter, Paul, Silas, James, and Apollos—Barnabas appears as a flickering flame . . . but, oh, how essential his light was. How warm . . . how inviting!

Journey with me through Chapter 4. The young, perse-
cuted assembly at Jerusalem was literally "under the gun."
If ever they needed encouragement, it was then. They
were backed to the wall and financially stripped. Many
were pressed, the needs were desperate. The comforter
from Cyprus spontaneously gave all he had. He sold a tract
of land and demonstrated that he was living for others by
bringing the proceeds to this band of believers (vv. 32-
37). That's what we might call: *encouragement in finances.*

The next time Barnabas appears, he's at it again! In
Chapter 11 the Body is growing and the Word is spreading
like a flame. It's too big for the leaders to handle. Assistance is needed: gifted assistance. What does Barnabas
do? He searches for and finds Saul of Tarsus (v. 25) who
was an outcast because of his former life. Not afraid to
stick his neck out for a new Christian who was suspect in
the eyes of the public, Barnabas took him by the hand and
brought him to Antioch. Before the entire assembly, the
"Son of Encouragement" gave his new friend a push into a
priority position . . . in fact, it was into the very place
where Barnabas himself had been experiencing remarkable blessing as a church leader (vv. 22-23, 26).

Without a thought of jealousy, he later allowed Saul to
take the leadership and set the pace for the first missionary
journey (Chapter 13). It is interesting to note that the
names were soon switched from "Barnabas . . . and Saul"
(13:1), to "Paul and Barnabas" (13:42). This is the su-
preme test. It takes a great person to recognize that a man
younger than he has God-given abilities and to encourage
him to move ahead with full support. This we might call:
encouragement of fellowship and followship.

The curtain comes down upon Barnabas' life in Chapter 15. Journey 2 is about to begin. He and Paul discuss the
possibility of taking John Mark, a young man who earlier
had chosen not to encounter the rigors of that first missionary journey (13:13). Can you imagine that discus-
sion?

"No," said Paul. "He failed once . . . he will again!"

"Yes," insisted Barnabas. "He can and will succeed with encouragement."

Paul would not withdraw his no vote. Barnabas stood his ground, believing in the young man's life, in spite of what happened before. Same style as always. You know the outcome (vv. 36-39). Barnabas demonstrated: *encouragement in spite of failure.*

Oh, the need for this ministry today! Is there some soul known to you in need of *financial* encouragement? A student off at school . . . a young couple up against it . . . a divorcee struggling to gain back self-acceptance . . . a forgotten servant of God laboring in an obscure and difficult ministry . . . ? Encourage generously!

Do you know of someone who could and should be promoted to a place of greater usefulness, but is presently in need of your companionship and confidence? Go to bat for him! Stand in his stead . . . give him a boost. He needs your *fellowship.* How about someone who is better qualified than yourself? You would be amazed at the blessing God would pour out upon you if you'd really back him with *fellowship.*

Then there are the failures. The Lots, the Samsons, the Jonahs, the Demases, the John Marks. Yes, they failed. They blew it. Are you big enough to extend a hand of encouragement and genuine love? Lift up the *failure* with encouragement. It pays off! It did in John's case. He wrote the Gospel of Mark and ultimately proved to be very useful to Paul's ministry (2 Timothy 4:11b).

To Henry Drummond's indictment, I suggest a solution. A new watchword for our times.

ENCOURAGEMENT!

Shout it out. Pass it around.

Conclusion

You can talk all you want about diamonds or dinosaur teeth or marble-sized pearls. Sure they're rare. Sure they're tough to find. You've got to tunnel under mountains, excavate ancient lakebeds, or dive to murky depths in mysterious lagoons.

But I submit that encouragement—genuine, warm-hearted, Christ-inspired encouragement—is an even more precious commodity than these. And infinitely more valuable.

Encouragement is awesome. Think about it: It has the capacity to lift a man's or woman's shoulders. To spark the flicker of a smile on the face of a discouraged child. To breathe fresh fire into the fading embers of a smoldering dream. To actually change the course of another human being's day . . . or week . . . or life.

That, my friend, is no small thing. But it doesn't stop there. Consistent, timely encouragement has the staggering magnetic power to draw an immortal soul to the God of hope. The One whose name is Wonderful Counselor.

Is it easy? Not on your life. It takes courage, tough-minded courage, to trust God, to believe in ourselves, and to reach a hand to others. But what a beautiful way to live. I know of no one more needed, more valuable, *more Christ-like,* than the person who is committed to encouragement. In spite of others' actions. Regardless of others' attitudes. It is the musical watchword that takes the grind out of living—*encouragement.*

Those of you who are living with Christ in your life will not be able to maintain this encouraging lifestyle unless the Spirit of God is given the controls and freedom to live His life through you. God gave us His Spirit so that He might come alongside and encourage us day after day. Please release yourself to Him so that you, in turn, can release yourself to others.

Those of you who do *not* claim to know Christ personally cannot expect to enter into the depths of these thoughts unless you turn, by faith, to the Son of God, Jesus our Lord. Only then can you receive the encouragement God promises His people. And only then can you give to others the kind of lasting encouragement that will not only ease hurts, but also change lives.

When David was "greatly distressed" (1 Samuel 30:6 KJV), nose-to-nose with death and heart-deep in discouragement, Scripture tells us that he *"encouraged himself in the LORD his God."*

David's Refuge is available to you . . . right now. No waiting. No appointment necessary.

And the Encourager is in.

Footnotes

1. From *Psalms of My Life* by Joseph Bayly, copyright 1969 by Tyndale House Publishers, Wheaton, Ill. Used by permission.

2. Bruce Larsen and Keith Miller, *The Edge of Adventure* (Waco, Tex.: Word Books, 1974), p. 156.

3. Dorothy Hsu, *Mending* (Elgin, Ill.: David C. Cook Publishing Co., 1979). Used by permission.

4. F. B. Meyer, *Christianity in Isaiah* (Grand Rapids: Zondervan Publishing House, 1950), p. 9.

5. Alexander Solzhenitsyn, *The Gulag Archipelago,* quoted in Philip Yancey, *Where Is God When It Hurts?* (Grand Rapids: Zondervan Publishing House, 1977), p. 51.

6. Henry W. Baker, "Art Thou Weary, Art Thou Languid?"

7. William Barclay, The Letter to the Hebrews, *The Daily Study Bible* (Edinburgh: The St. Andrew Press, 1955), pp. 137-138.

8. Reprinted by permission from the Christian Medical Society Journal, Vol. XII Number 2 1981. The Christian Medical Society is a fellowship of Christian physicians and dentists representing Jesus Christ in and through medicine and dentistry.

9. Richard H. Seume, *Shoes for the Road* (Chicago: Moody Press, 1974), p. 117.

10. Stephen Pile, *The Incomplete Book of Failures* (New York: E. P. Dutton, 1979), pp. 165-167.

11. Fanny Crosby, "Rescue the Perishing."